good answers
to tough questions

About Physical Disabilities

Written by Joy Berry

 CHILDRENS PRESS ®

CHICAGO

Managing Editor: Lana Eberhard

Copy Editor: Annette Gooch

Contributing Editors: Margie Austin, John Bilitch, Ph.D.,
Libby Byers, Ilene Frommer, James Gough, M.D.,
Dan Gurney, Charles Pengra, Ph.D.

Art Direction: Communication Graphics

Designer: Jennifer Wiezel

Illustration Designer: Bartholomew

Inking Artist: Ann Clements

Lettering Artist: Linda Hanney

Coloring Artist: Alyson Butler

Typography and Production: Communication Graphics

Published by Childrens Press
in cooperation with Living Skills Press

This book can answer the following questions:
- What is a physical disability?
- What causes physical disabilities?
- What are the ways a person's body can be disabled?
- How do people with physical disabilities function?
- How do people feel about the physically disabled?
- How should you act around the physically disabled?

Every person is *unique*. The word unique means **different**. It means **unlike any other**. To say that a person is unique is to say that he or she is different from any other person. It is to say that he or she is one of a kind.

Because every person is one of a kind, no one person can ever be replaced. This makes each person extremely valuable.

One thing that makes a person one of a kind is his or her **physical characteristics**. Physical characteristics are things such as

- hair and skin color,
- facial features,
- body size and shape, and
- the way the body functions.

Physical characteristics determine what a person looks like. They also determine what a person can or cannot do.

Some physical characteristics hinder people from doing some of the things most people normally do, such as

- seeing,
- hearing,
- talking,
- smelling,
- touching,
- holding,
- reaching,
- walking,
- running,
- skipping, and
- jumping.

A physical characteristic that hinders a person from doing something most people normally do is called a *physical disability*.

Physical disabilities hinder people from doing certain things. However, they do not hinder people from doing the most important things in life such as

- thinking,
- feeling,
- loving,
- caring,
- communicating,
- giving,
- taking,
- learning,
- growing,
- progressing, and
- succeeding.

There are several ways people can become physically disabled. **Some people are born with physical disabilities.**

Some babies inherit physical disabilities from their mothers or fathers.

Some babies **develop** physical disabilities because of something that happened to them before they were born.

Some babies become disabled because they are injured while being born.

Some people become physically disabled after they are born. Sometimes serious accidents cause people to become physically disabled.

Some people become physically disabled because they have been severely wounded.

Some people become physically disabled because of certain serious illnesses.

I KNOW A WOMAN WHO HAD **POLIO** WHEN SHE WAS A CHILD AND NOW SHE CAN'T MOVE HER RIGHT ARM AND LEG.

COMMON ILLNESSES SUCH AS COLDS AND THE FLU DO NOT CAUSE PHYSICAL DISABILITIES. THE RARE ILLNESSES THAT CAUSE A PERSON TO BECOME PHYSICALLY DISABLED HAPPEN VERY SELDOM AND ONLY TO A FEW PEOPLE.

Sometimes the *aging process* causes people to become physically disabled.

A person's body can be disabled in various ways. Some people have parts of their bodies missing.

A person who is born with a missing limb, such as an arm, hand, leg, or foot, is called a **congenital amputee**. A person who has had a limb removed from his or her body is called an **amputee**.

Some people have body parts that are misshaped.

A misshapen body part is called a **deformity**. Sometimes the word **crippled** is used to describe a deformed body part.

Some people have body parts that move uncontrollably or that do not function normally.

Muscular spasms can cause body parts to move uncontrollably. Sometimes the word *spastic* is used to describe such body movements.

Some people have body parts that do not move at all.

Muscular dystrophy weakens the muscles and prevents them from moving. The word *paralyzed* is used to describe a body or body part that cannot move at all. A person whose legs are both paralyzed is said to be *paraplegic*. A person whose legs and arms are paralyzed is said to be *quadriplegic*.

Some amputees have body parts such as arms, hands, legs, or feet missing. These people often replace their missing body parts with specially made devices. An artificial replacement for a missing body part is called a **prosthesis**.

Some prostheses look like the body parts they are meant to replace. For example, some artificial limbs look like human arms, hands, legs, or feet. Other prostheses do not. For example, a two-part hook worn in place of a hand does not look like a hand.

A prosthesis is usually strapped onto the body. Sometimes it can be manipulated by other functioning body parts.

A prosthesis can help an amputee do things that would normally be done by the body part that is missing.

Some people with physical disabilities involving their feet or legs have a difficult time walking. Some use special physical aids to help them get around.

Often these people use physical aids such as
- braces,
- canes,
- crutches,
- walkers, or
- wheelchairs.

Some people with physical disabilities affecting their hands or arms have a difficult time handling things.

Often these people use their mouths and feet to pick up and hold things. They also use their heads and bodies to move things.

Some people have almost no control over their bodies and need help to dress, eat, and do other everyday things.

Often these people need to be strapped to their wheelchairs so they will not fall out when they are up during the day. They also need to be strapped into their beds so they will not fall out when they are sleeping.

Physical disabilities can make it difficult for people to move or control certain parts of their bodies. However, physical disabilities do not keep people from doing the most important things in life. Physically disabled people have the ability to

- think,
- feel,
- love,
- care,
- communicate,
- give,
- take,
- learn,
- grow,
- progress, and
- succeed.

To accomplish these things, people with physically disabled bodies use their minds and the parts of their bodies that function normally in unique and creative ways.

Some people are **curious** whenever they see a physically disabled person. They wonder:

- What is wrong with the person?
- How did the person's body become that way?
- How does the person do everyday things that are necessary to survive and be happy?
- What would it be like to be disabled in the same way as that person?

Some people feel *uncomfortable* around a person who is physically disabled.
- They do not know how they should act.
- They do not know how the disabled person will act.
- They are worried that something strange might happen.

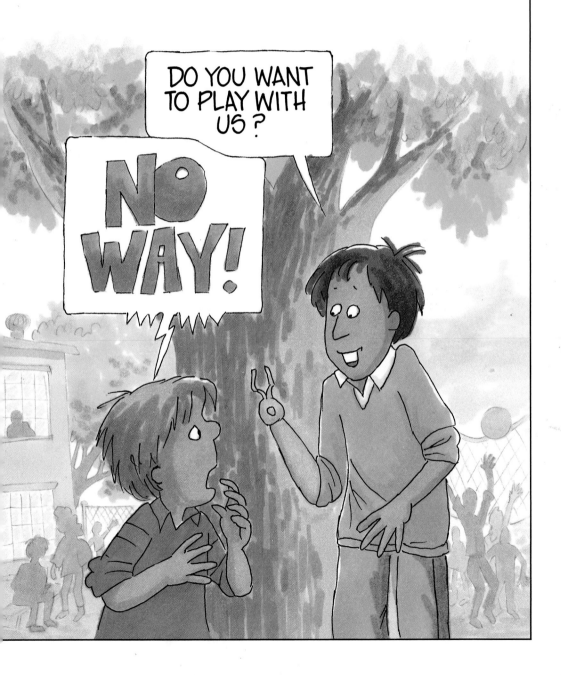

Some people feel *afraid* around a person who is physically disabled. They think that a disability is contagious (something that can be transmitted to them).

Some people feel *vulnerable* around a person who is physically disabled. Seeing a disabled person reminds them that something could happen to make them become disabled. This is a frightening thought for people who are not sure whether they could survive or be happy if they were disabled.

Some people feel **superior** around a person who is physically disabled. These people think that their bodies are more efficient and better-looking than a disabled person's body.

Some people feel *pity* for anyone who is physically disabled. This is because they do not think that disabled people can do the things that are necessary to survive and enjoy life.

Unfortunately, some people's ignorance, feelings, and attitudes keep them from relating to those with physical disabilities.

This is not good because it
- causes disabled people to be left out of groups and activities,
- keeps people from sharing what they have to give to others, and
- keeps people from receiving what they deserve to receive from each other.

In addition, when people avoid those who are physically disabled, they deprive themselves of relationships that might enhance and enrich their lives.

It will be easier for you to relate to a physically disabled person if you remember these things:

- Every person has abilities and disabilities that contribute to his or her identity and purpose in life.
- No one is superior or inferior to any other person.
- Each person is one of a kind and valuable in his or her own way.

If you are curious about someone who is physically disabled, you need to
- ask questions,
- talk to someone who knows the disabled person, and
- choose a person who will give you correct information.

Often you will discover that it is appropriate for you to talk directly to the disabled person to have more of your questions answered.

When you see a physically disabled person, avoid
- staring or pointing at the person, and
- making fun of or saying unkind things about the person.

When you are around a physically disabled person, it is important to
- act the same way you would around any other person,
- be kind and respectful, and
- focus your attention on all the things the person **can** do, rather than on what the person **cannot** do.

It is important to remember this:

Physical disabilities are only as limiting as people allow them to be.